MY FIRST
BMX
RACE

My First BMX Race Copyright

THIS BOOK IS DEDICATED TO MY BOY SIRIAN, THE BIGGEST LIGHT AND INSPIRATION IN MY LIFE. AND TO THE BEAUTIFUL KELLY MC ‿

-AND A SPECIAL SHOUT OUT TO **STRIDER**®

TONIGHT
WAS MY FIRST RACE
AT THE
BMX TRACK

HELMET

PADS

GLOVES

I HAD TO PUT ON MY SPECIAL GEAR

THEN I GOT TO PRACTICE ON THE COURSE.

I HAD TO STAY INSIDE THE CONES,

AND WATCH OUT FOR MY **FRIENDS**

AFTER WARM UP, IT WAS TIME TO RACE

WE GOT IN OUR PLACE AT THE STARTING LINE

AND I TOOK OFF WHEN THE MAN YELLED, "GO!"

I HAD TO **BALANCE** ON MY BIKE!

AND GO AS **FAST** AS I COULD!

I FELT SO BRAVE!

I RODE OVER THE HILLS, AND AROUND SOME BIG TURNS

MY FAMILY CHEERED ME ON,
THEN I CROSSED THE FINISH LINE!

I GOT 3RD PLACE AT MY FIRST RACE!

I GOT A MEDAL AND WORE IT AROUND MY NECK

I HAD SO MUCH FUN!

I CAN'T WAIT TO RACE AGAIN!

THE END

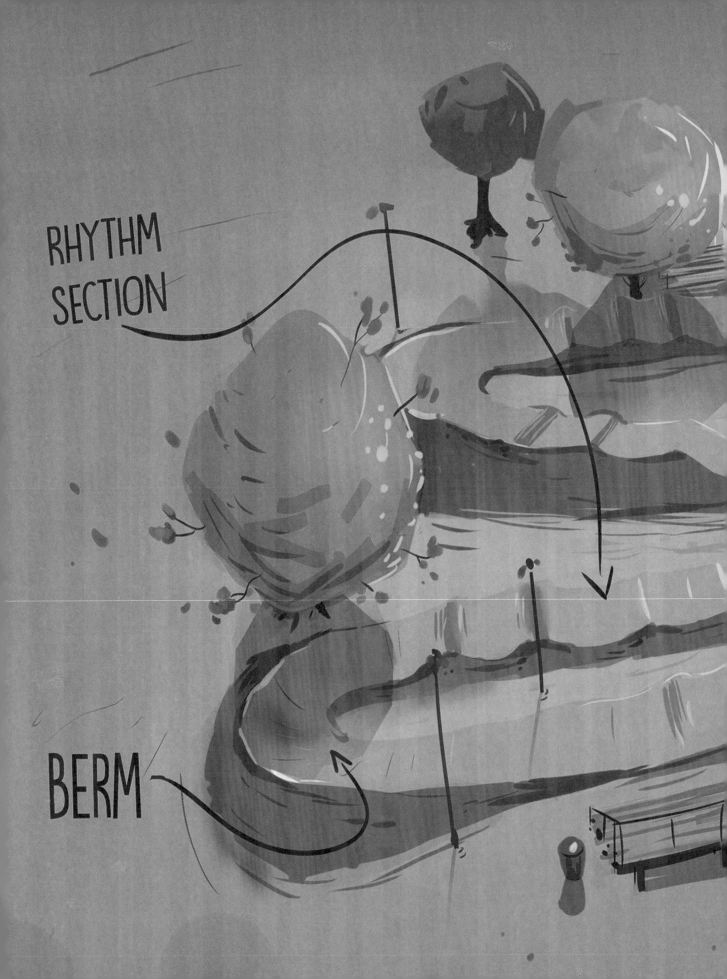

RHYTHM
SECTION

BERM

STARTING HILL

ME

ILLUSTRATOR

Edward is a professional snacker, when he's not snacking you can find him drawing or riding his bicycle.

Visit: ArtofEdwardDennis.com

 @EduardoDenniz

AUTHOR

Brittny grew up in Arizona where she loves to ride dirt bikes. When she's not writing, she loves to be outside having adventures!

Connect with Brittny:
www.LiLRacerBook.com

 @LilRacerBooks